This Book Belongs To:

2019/2020

School Calendar

Aug 2019	Sep 2019	Oct 2019	Nov 2019	Dec 2019	Jan 2020
1 Th	1 Su	1 Tu	1 Fr	1 Su	1 We New Year's Day
2 Fr	2 Mo Labor Day	2 We	2 Sa	2 Mo	2 Th
3 Sa	3 Tu	3 Th	3 Su	3 Tu	3 Fr
4 Su	4 We	4 Fr	4 Mo	4 We	4 Sa
5 Mo	5 Th	5 Sa	5 Tu	5 Th	5 Su
6 Tu	6 Fr	6 Su	6 We	6 Fr	6 Mo
7 We	7 Sa	7 Mo	7 Th	7 Sa	7 Tu
8 Th	8 Su	8 Tu	8 Fr	8 Su	8 We
9 Fr	9 Mo	9 We	9 Sa	9 Mo	9 Th
10 Sa	10 Tu	10 Th	10 Su	10 Tu	10 Fr
11 Su	11 We	11 Fr	11 Mo Veterans Day	11 We	11 Sa
12 Mo	12 Th	12 Sa	12 Tu	12 Th	12 Su
13 Tu	13 Fr	13 Su	13 We	13 Fr	13 Mo
14 We	14 Sa	14 Mo Columbus Day	14 Th	14 Sa	14 Tu
15 Th	15 Su	15 Tu	15 Fr	15 Su	15 We
16 Fr	16 Mo	16 We	16 Sa	16 Mo	16 Th
17 Sa	17 Tu	17 Th	17 Su	17 Tu	17 Fr
18 Su	18 We	18 Fr	18 Mo	18 We	18 Sa
19 Mo	19 Th	19 Sa	19 Tu	19 Th	19 Su
20 Tu	20 Fr	20 Su	20 We	20 Fr	20 Mo M. L. King Day
21 We	21 Sa	21 Mo	21 Th	21 Sa	21 Tu
22 Th	22 Su	22 Tu	22 Fr	22 Su	22 We
23 Fr	23 Mo	23 We	23 Sa	23 Mo	23 Th
24 Sa	24 Tu	24 Th	24 Su	24 Tu	24 Fr
25 Su	25 We	25 Fr	25 Mo	25 We Christmas Day	25 Sa
26 Mo	26 Th	26 Sa	26 Tu	26 Th	26 Su
27 Tu	27 Fr	27 Su	27 We	27 Fr	27 Mo
28 We	28 Sa	28 Mo	28 Th Thanksgiving Day	28 Sa	28 Tu
29 Th	29 Su	29 Tu	29 Fr	29 Su	29 We
30 Fr	30 Mo	30 We	30 Sa	30 Mo	30 Th
31 Sa		31 Th		31 Tu	31 Fr

Feb 2020	Mar 2020	Apr 2020	May 2020	Jun 2020	Jul 2020
1 Sa	1 Su	1 We	1 Fr	1 Mo	1 We
2 Su	2 Mo	2 Th	2 Sa	2 Tu	2 Th
3 Mo	3 Tu	3 Fr	3 Su	3 We	3 Fr Indep. Day (obs.)
4 Tu	4 We	4 Sa	4 Mo	4 Th	4 Sa Independence Day
5 We	5 Th	5 Su	5 Tu	5 Fr	5 Su
6 Th	6 Fr	6 Mo	6 We	6 Sa	6 Mo
7 Fr	7 Sa	7 Tu	7 Th	7 Su	7 Tu
8 Sa	8 Su	8 We	8 Fr	8 Mo	8 We
9 Su	9 Mo	9 Th	9 Sa	9 Tu	9 Th
10 Mo	10 Tu	10 Fr	10 Su	10 We	10 Fr
11 Tu	11 We	11 Sa	11 Mo	11 Th	11 Sa
12 We	12 Th	12 Su	12 Tu	12 Fr	12 Su
13 Th	13 Fr	13 Mo	13 We	13 Sa	13 Mo
14 Fr	14 Sa	14 Tu	14 Th	14 Su	14 Tu
15 Sa	15 Su	15 We	15 Fr	15 Mo	15 We
16 Su	16 Mo	16 Th	16 Sa	16 Tu	16 Th
17 Mo Presidents' Day	17 Tu	17 Fr	17 Su	17 We	17 Fr
18 Tu	18 We	18 Sa	18 Mo	18 Th	18 Sa
19 We	19 Th	19 Su	19 Tu	19 Fr	19 Su
20 Th	20 Fr	20 Mo	20 We	20 Sa	20 Mo
21 Fr	21 Sa	21 Tu	21 Th	21 Su	21 Tu
22 Sa	22 Su	22 We	22 Fr	22 Mo	22 We
23 Su	23 Mo	23 Th	23 Sa	23 Tu	23 Th
24 Mo	24 Tu	24 Fr	24 Su	24 We	24 Fr
25 Tu	25 We	25 Sa	25 Mo Memorial Day	25 Th	25 Sa
26 We	26 Th	26 Su	26 Tu	26 Fr	26 Su
27 Th	27 Fr	27 Mo	27 We	27 Sa	27 Mo
28 Fr	28 Sa	28 Tu	28 Th	28 Su	28 Tu
29 Sa	29 Su	29 We	29 Fr	29 Mo	29 We
	30 Mo	30 Th	30 Sa	30 Tu	30 Th
	31 Tu		31 Su		31 Fr

Made in the USA
Monee, IL
09 August 2021